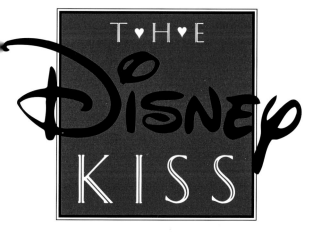

T♥H♥E

KISS

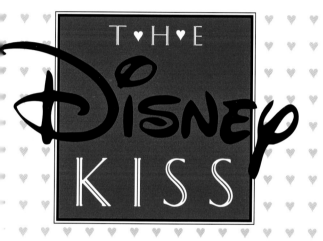

T · H · E

Disney

KISS

HYPERION

NEW YORK

Library of Congress Cataloging-In-Publication Data
ISBN 0-7868-6178-9

DESIGNED BY CLAUDYNE BIANCO

First Edition
10 9 8 7 6 5 4 3 2 1

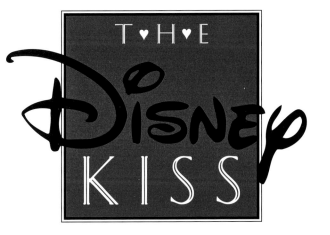

THE ♥ Disney ♥ KISS

BRAVE LITTLE TAILOR
1938

LIKE MANY DISNEY SHORTS, *BRAVE LITTLE TAILOR* IS BASED ON A GRIMM'S FAIRY TALE. IT FEATURES MICKEY IN A TRADITIONAL ROLE, AS THE HUMBLE UNDERDOG WHO PERSEVERES IN THE FACE OF SEEMINGLY IMPOSSIBLE ODDS. IN THIS CASE, HE MUST VANQUISH THE GIANT WHO HAS BEEN TERRORIZING THE COUNTRYSIDE. HIS REWARD WILL BE THE HAND OF THE FAIR PRINCESS MINNIE, SUFFICIENT MOTIVATION FOR ANY BRAVE YOUNG MAN.

IN DUTCH
1946

IN DUTCH COMBINES THE THEMES OF THE BOY WHO CRIED "WOLF!" AND OF THE BOY WHO PUT HIS FINGER IN THE DIKE. EARLY ON IN THE SHORT, PLUTO AND DINAH ARE EXPELLED FROM THE TOWN AFTER A SERIES OF MISHAPS, WHICH END IN THEM SETTING OFF THE DIKE-BREACH ALARM BELL. FAR FROM THE TOWN, THEY DISCOVER THAT THERE IS INDEED A HOLE IN THE DIKE. DINAH SEALS THE LEAK WHILE PLUTO ALERTS THE TOWN, AND THE TWO EXILES BECOME THE HEROES OF THE DAY.

SNOW WHITE AND THE SEVEN DWARFS

1937

WALT DISNEY REALIZED EARLY ON
THAT THE DWARFS WERE CRUCIAL
TO THE SUCCESS OF THE MOVIE.
SNOW WHITE IS A LOVABLE
HEROINE, BUT THE DWARFS WOULD
BE RESPONSIBLE FOR PROVIDING
THE COMEDY AND HUMAN INTEREST.
EACH DWARF DEVELOPED A DIS-
TINCT PERSONALITY BASED ON THE
DRAWINGS AND VOICES THAT
BROUGHT HIM TO LIFE. IT DOES NOT
TAKE LONG FOR THE DWARFS TO
FALL IN LOVE WITH SNOW WHITE,
AND DOC IS ONE OF THE FIRST TO
LINE UP FOR A GOOD-
BYE KISS BEFORE MARCHING
OFF TO WORK.

SLEEPING BEAUTY
1959

THIS DISNEY PRINCE HAS A FAR
MEATIER ROLE THAN THE LEADING
MAN IN EITHER *SNOW WHITE* OR
CINDERELLA. CONSEQUENTLY, HIS
CHARACTER HAD TO BE PORTRAYED
IN MORE DETAIL. PRINCE PHILLIP IS
EVERYTHING YOU WOULD EXPECT:
GENTLE, GOOD-NATURED, WELL-
SPOKEN, COURTEOUS, ROMANTIC
AND, ABOVE ALL, COURAGEOUS.
WHAT'S MORE, THESE CHARACTERIS-
TICS ARE ALL BLENDED TOGETHER
TO CREATE A CONVINCING, FULLY
ROUNDED PERSONALITY. WHEN HE
KISSES PRINCESS AURORA FOR THE
FIRST TIME, THE WHOLE CASTLE
WAKES UP AND CELEBRATES.

DONALD'S DILEMMA
1947

THE DILEMMA IN THIS SHORT REALLY IS DAISY'S. AFTER BEING STRUCK ON THE HEAD BY A FLOWER POT, DONALD UNDERGOES TWO DRAMATIC CHANGES: HE BECOMES THE WORLD'S FINEST CROONER AND HE NO LONGER RECOGNIZES HIS LOVE. DAISY'S SOLUTION IS TO DROP AN EVEN HEAVIER POT ON HIS HEAD, WITH THE DESIRED EFFECT. DONALD IS RESTORED TO HIS OLD SELF. HIS SINGING CAREER IS RUINED, BUT HE AND DAISY ARE REUNITED IN A LENGTHY KISS.

BEAUTY AND THE BEAST
1991

THE ORIGINS OF DISNEY'S *BEAUTY AND THE BEAST* CAN BE TRACED BACK TO THE EARLY 1950s WHEN WALT DISNEY FIRST DISCUSSED POSSIBILITIES FOR THE STORY. THE STUDIO MADE SOME REVISIONS TO THE ORIGINAL STORY TO MAKE IT LESS ABOUT BEAUTY, AND MORE ABOUT THE BEAST. THE KEYS TO THE BEAST'S COMPLEX CHARACTER ARE HIS EYES. THESE WINDOWS TO THE SOUL ALLOW OTHERS TO SEE THAT HE HAS TRUE LOVE IN HIS HEART AND CAN PROVE HE IS MORE THAN A BEAST.

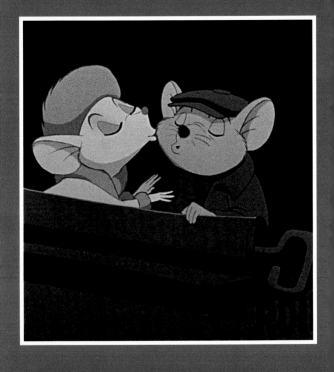

THE RESCUERS DOWN UNDER

1990

A SEQUEL TO THE 1977 RELEASE *THE RESCUERS*, THIS MOVIE OFTEN IS VIEWED AS ONE OF DISNEY'S MORE MODEST ANIMATED FEATURES. NONETHELESS, *THE RESCUERS DOWN UNDER* HAS ITS MOMENTS OF TRIUMPH. AMONG THEM ARE CODY'S GLORIOUS FLIGHTS ASTRIDE THE GOLDEN EAGLE, MARAHUTE. THE MAJESTY OF THESE IS UNDERSCORED BY THE BUMPY RIDES THAT BERNARD AND BIANCA MUST ENDURE ABOARD WILBUR, THE GREAT ALBATROSS WHO SERVES AS BOTH STAFF AND VEHICLE OF ALBATROSS AIR CHARTER SERVICE.

POCAHONTAS
1995

NATURE BECOMES A CENTRAL
CHARACTER IN *POCAHONTAS*,
EMBODYING NATIVE AMERICAN
PHILOSOPHY, BEAUTY,
AND THE SYMBOLISM OF
POCAHONTAS' WORLD.
THE CONTRAST BETWEEN
POCAHONTAS' SPIRITUALITY
AND JOHN SMITH'S WORLDLINESS
FUELS MUCH OF THE FILM'S
DRAMA AND ACTION.
THEIR LOVE FOR EACH OTHER
EMPHASIZES THE THEMES
OF INDEPENDENCE, TOLERANCE,
AND OVERCOMING IGNORANCE.

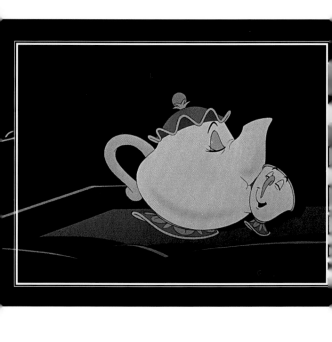

BEAUTY AND THE BEAST
1991

THE MAKERS OF *BEAUTY AND THE BEAST* PAID PARTICULAR ATTENTION TO ITS VISUAL PRESENTATION. THEY CHOSE A RICH, COLORFUL STYLE DESIGNED TO SUGGEST BOTH THE FILM'S EUROPEAN SETTING AND THE QUALITY OF THE DISNEY ANIMATED CLASSICS. TECHNOLOGICAL ADVANCES GAVE THE ARTISTS AN ALMOST UNLIMITED PALETTE, WITH SEVERAL OF THE MAIN CHARACTERS USING AS MANY AS SEVENTEEN PAINT COLORS AND SEVEN DIFFERENT COLORS OF INK OUTLINE. MRS. POTTS OFTEN HAD CAUSE TO BLUSH IN THE FILM, WHEN HER YOUNG SON CHIP ASKED NAIVE BUT EMBARRASSING QUESTIONS, AND HER ROUGED CHEEKS WERE CREATED WITH A SOPHISTICATED BLENDING TECHNIQUE, PIONEERED FOR THIS FILM.

LADY AND THE TRAMP
1955

LADY AND THE TRAMP WAS A LONG TIME IN THE MAKING, WITH SEVERAL VERSIONS DATING AS FAR BACK AS 1936. THE FILM DEPARTED FROM THE NORM IN TWO WAYS: IT WAS THE FIRST ANIMATED FEATURE TO BE MADE IN CINEMASCOPE, AND IT WAS THE FIRST STORY *NOT* BASED ON A PUBLISHED BOOK. IN THE FILM'S MOST MEMORABLE SCENE, LADY AND TRAMP LOVINGLY SHARE THEIR FIRST KISS OVER A PLATE OF SPAGHETTI *ESPECIALLE*.

ALADDIN
1992

FREEDOM IS AN IMPOR-
TANT THEME IN
ALADDIN, A FILM IN
WHICH VIRTUALLY
EVERYONE IS TRAPPED
BY SOMETHING.
JASMINE AND HER
FATHER ARE BOUND BY
A LAW REQUIRING HER
TO MARRY A PRINCE.
JAFAR FEELS TRAPPED
AS LONG AS HE IS SUB-
ORDINATE TO THE
SULTAN. AND ALADDIN
IS AS IMPRISONED BY
HIS SOCIAL SITUATION
AS THE GENIE IS BY THE
LAMP.

PINOCCHIO
1940

BECAUSE PINOCCHIO WAS LARGELY A BLANK CHARACTER, DISNEY ANIMATORS SURROUNDED HIM WITH LIVELY, FLAMBOYANT FIGURES, INCLUDING THE LIKABLE FIGARO AND CLEO. INTERESTINGLY ENOUGH, THE FILM'S MOST SIGNIFICANT CHARACTER, JIMINY CRICKET, WAS VIRTUALLY NONEXISTENT IN THE CARLO COLLODI TALE ON WHICH *PINOCCHIO* IS BASED. COLLODI PRESENTED THE CRICKET AS A NAMELESS INSECT, SQUASHED BY THE PUPPET-BOY AFTER ADVISING HIM TO CHANGE HIS WAYS. EXPANDING THE CRICKET'S ROLE WAS A BRILLIANT MOVE THAT ADVANCED THE MOVIE'S PLOT AND CREATED ONE OF DISNEY'S MOST POPULAR CHARACTERS.

THE LITTLE MERMAID
1989

ARIEL'S INDEPENDENCE AND DETER-
MINATION MARKED HER AS THE
FIRST OF A NEW BREED OF DISNEY-
FEATURE HEROINES. THE SPUNKY
TEENAGER KNOWS EXACTLY WHAT
SHE WANTS AND HAS COMPLETE
CONFIDENCE IN HER ABILITY TO
CARRY OUT HER PLANS. AS WITH
MANY A TEENAGER, THAT CONFI-
DENCE OFTEN IS ILL PLACED. YET
ARIEL IS PORTRAYED SO MASTERFUL-
LY THAT, RATHER THAN DETRACT
FROM OUR HEROINE, THIS TRAIT
ONLY MAKES HER MORE ENDEARING.
IN THE END, HER WISH COMES TRUE,
AND SHE WEDS THE MAN OF HER
DREAMS, PRINCE ERIC.

MICKEY'S CHRISTMAS CAROL
1983

THE FIRST BILL-TOPPING ANIMATED FEATURETTE IN YEARS, *MICKEY'S CHRISTMAS CAROL* SAW MANY OF THE CLASSIC DISNEY CHARACTERS IN DICKENSIAN GUISE. GOOFY TURNS IN A MEMORABLE PERFORMANCE AS MARLEY'S GHOST. THE GHOSTS OF CHRISTMAS PAST, PRESENT, AND FUTURE ARE PLAYED RESPECTIVELY BY JIMINY CRICKET, WILLIE THE GIANT, AND PETE. OF COURSE, NO ONE FEATURED SO PROMINENTLY AS SCROOGE. THIS DUCK HAS NEVER BEEN GENEROUS ABOUT ANYTHING, AND THE LIMELIGHT IS NO EXCEPTION AS HE DANCES WITH HIS YOUTHFUL SWEETHEART, ISABEL, PLAYED BY DAISY.

THE BLACK CAULDRON

1985

BASED ON LLOYD ALEXANDER'S FIVE *CHRONICLES OF PRYDAIN* BOOKS, *THE BLACK CAULDRON* IS DISNEY'S FIRST ANIMATED FEATURE TO BE FILMED IN 70 MM SINCE *SLEEPING BEAUTY*. NOTABLE FOR ITS MIXTURE OF ANIMATION STYLES, *THE BLACK CAULDRON* INCLUDES SOME EXPERIMENTAL SEQUENCES THAT ARE AMONG THE BEST PIECES OF ANIMATION EVER CREATED. CHARACTERS RANGE FROM THE REALISTIC TARAN AND EILONWY TO THE PURELY CARTOON GURGI AND FFLEWDDUR FFLAM.

SNOW WHITE AND THE SEVEN DWARFS

1937

GRUMPY BECAME ONE OF THE
FILM'S MOST COMPLEX AND THREE-
DIMENSIONAL CHARACTERS, WHO
TRANSFORMS FROM A DYSPEPTIC,
PESSIMISTIC MISOGYNIST TO A
LOYAL, LOVING FRIEND. HE IS THE
LAST TO FALL IN LOVE WITH SNOW
WHITE, AND WHEN HE DOES, IS THE
FIRST TO WANT TO SAVE HER FROM
THE WICKED QUEEN.

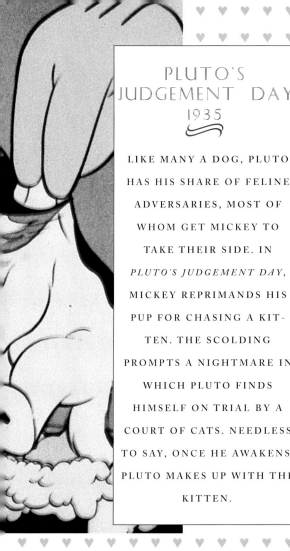

PLUTO'S JUDGEMENT DAY

1935

LIKE MANY A DOG, PLUTO HAS HIS SHARE OF FELINE ADVERSARIES, MOST OF WHOM GET MICKEY TO TAKE THEIR SIDE. IN *PLUTO'S JUDGEMENT DAY*, MICKEY REPRIMANDS HIS PUP FOR CHASING A KITTEN. THE SCOLDING PROMPTS A NIGHTMARE IN WHICH PLUTO FINDS HIMSELF ON TRIAL BY A COURT OF CATS. NEEDLESS TO SAY, ONCE HE AWAKENS, PLUTO MAKES UP WITH THE KITTEN.

BAMBI
1942

THE SERIOUSNESS OF ITS SUBJECT
MATTER SET *BAMBI* APART FROM
EARLIER DISNEY PRODUCTIONS AND
DETERMINED THE WAY ITS
CHARACTERS WOULD BE DRAWN.
THE STORYLINE REQUIRED THAT
THE ANIMALS BE PORTRAYED IN A
NATURAL MANNER; TO TREAT THEM
AS CARTOONS WOULD DESTROY THE
DRAMA. THE RESULT WAS A MOVIE
THAT TODAY IS WIDELY REGARDED
AS A MASTERPIECE FOR ITS
INCREDIBLE, NATURALISTIC DETAIL.

SHANGHAIED
1934

MINNIE HAS APPEARED IN A TOTAL
OF SEVENTY DISNEY SHORTS,
THOUGH NEVER IN A STARRING
ROLE. INSTEAD, THESE EARLY FILMS
SEE HER MOST OFTEN CAST AS A
FEEDER, A CHARACTER WHOSE PRI-
MARY PURPOSE IS TO ALLOW THE
HERO TO SHINE. IN *SHANGHAIED*,
MINNIE IS HELD PRISONER BY
CAPTAIN PEG LEG PETE. ARMED
WITH A STUFFED SWORDFISH TORN
FROM ITS MOUNTING, MICKEY
COMES TO THE RESCUE, PREVAILS
OVER THE NEFARIOUS CREW, AND
SAILS BACK TO PORT WITH HIS
LEADING LADY.

THE LION KING
1994

THE EARLIEST DRAFTS OF *THE LION KING* DATE BACK TO 1989, WHEN THE MOVIE WAS CALLED *KING OF THE JUNGLE*. DISNEY STUDIO MEMBERS TRAVELED TO EAST AFRICA TO GET A SENSE OF THE SPECTACULAR LANDSCAPE, WILDLIFE, AND CULTURE THAT WOULD SHAPE THIS FILM. THE FILM IS ROOTED ENTIRELY IN NATURE AND FEATURES AN ALL-ANIMAL CAST. THE RUNNING THEME IN THE STORY IS RESPONSIBILITY, AND IT IS NALA, SIMBA'S CHILDHOOD SWEETHEART, WHO HELPS HIM REALIZE HE MUST GO BACK TO THE PRIDE AND CLAIM HIS RIGHTFUL PLACE AS KING.

PETER PAN
1953

IN NEVER LAND, WENDY ASSUMES
THE ROLE OF MOTHER TO THE LOST
BOYS AND TO HER OWN BROTHERS,
JOHN AND MICHAEL. EVEN SO, SHE IS
MUCH MORE OF A CHILD THAN MOST
DISNEY ANIMATED HEROINES.
INDEED, ONE GETS THE SENSE THAT
SHE IS ACTING THE ROLE OF
MOTHER RATHER THAN
LIVING IT. PURPOSELY DEPICTED AS
ORDINARY, WENDY'S PORTRAYAL
EMPHASIZES THE FANTASTIC NATURE
OF PETER'S PERSONALITY AND OF
THE ADVENTURES THEY ALL SHARE.

SLEEPING BEAUTY
1959

ONE OF THE GREAT CLASSIC FAIRY TALES TO BE FILMED BY DISNEY, *SLEEPING BEAUTY* WAS IN PRODUCTION FOR ABOUT A DECADE. ON THE STRENGTH OF ITS ARTWORK ALONE, THE FILM REPRESENTS AN IMAGINATIVE LEAP FORWARD. AMONG ITS MOST BRILLIANT CREATIONS ARE MALEFICENT'S GOONS. IN ADDITION TO THEIR ROLE IN THE PLOT, THESE INCOMPETENT SIDEKICKS DILUTE THE SCREEN FORCE OF THE WICKED FAIRY'S EVIL. IN THE FINAL SCENE, PRINCESS AURORA AND PRINCE PHILLIP WALTZ TOGETHER AS AURORA'S DRESS CONTINUES TO CHANGE FROM BLUE TO PINK.

DONALD'S CRIME
1945

THE 1940s WERE FULL OF GREAT
MOMENTS FOR DONALD DUCK, WHO
HAS APPEARED IN FAR MORE
MOVIES THAN MICKEY MOUSE. IN
DONALD'S CRIME, HE RAIDS HIS
NEPHEWS' PIGGY BANK TO TAKE
DAISY OUT ON A DATE. AFTER
REPLACING THE MONEY, DONALD
DISCOVERS THAT HE HAS OVERPAID
BY A NICKEL. WHILE TRYING TO
EXTRACT THE EXTRA FIVE CENTS,
HE IS CAUGHT AND REPRIMANDED
BY THE VOCIFEROUS TRIO.

THE ARISTOCATS
1970

AFTER A LONG STINT AS THE
VILLAINS IN WALT DISNEY FILMS,
CATS BECAME THE HEROES IN *THE
ARISTOCATS*. DUCHESS AND HER
THREE KITTENS ARE ADORED BY
THEIR MISTRESS, THE WEALTHY
MADAME BONFAMILLE, AND BY HER
ELDERLY ATTORNEY, GEORGES
HAUTECOURT. ONCE DESCRIBED AS
"THE OLDEST LAWYER IN THE
WORLD," GEORGES IS EVERYBODY'S
FAVORITE GRANDFATHER. HIS AFFEC-
TION FOR THE CATS IS APPARENT IN
HIS DELIGHT AT DRAFTING A WILL IN
THEIR FAVOR.

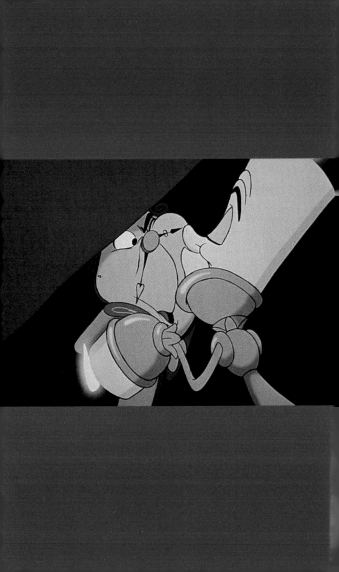

BEAUTY AND THE BEAST
1991

THE ORIGINS OF THIS MOVIE CAN BE TRACED BACK AT LEAST FORTY YEARS, TO INITIAL DISCUSSIONS BETWEEN WALT DISNEY AND OTHER MEMBERS OF HIS CREATIVE TEAM. THE PROJECT WAS SHELVED BECAUSE OF PROBLEMS PRESENTED BY THE STORY'S DARKER SECOND HALF, WHEN BEAUTY IS IMPRIS-ONED BY THE BEAST. THE SOLUTION CAME FROM EXECUTIVE PRODUCER AND LYRICIST HOWARD ASHMAN, WHO TRANSFORMED THE CASTLE'S ENCHANTED OBJECTS INTO CHARAC-TERS WITH THEIR OWN PERSONALITIES, VOICES, AND SONGS. TWO OF THE BEST-LOVED OBJECTS, COGSWORTH AND LUMIERE, ARE ALSO THE BEST OF FRIENDS, DESPITE THEIR CONTRASTING PERSONALITIES.

THE LITTLE MERMAID
1989

DISNEY ANIMATORS WELCOMED THE OPPORTUNITY TO CREATE *THE LITTLE MERMAID*, WHOSE UNDERWATER SETTING FREED THEM FROM THE CONSTRAINTS OF GRAVITY. UNDER THE SEA, THEIR CHARACTERS COULD SWIM, DIVE, AND TWIRL IN AN ATMOSPHERE MADE POSSIBLE ONLY BY EXTENSIVE SPECIAL EFFECTS. IN FACT, ALMOST 80 PERCENT OF THE MOVIE'S SCENES REQUIRED SOME EFFECTS WORK, REPRESENTING PERHAPS THE STRONGEST RELIANCE ON SPECIAL EFFECTS SINCE *FANTASIA*. ANIMATORS HAD TO USE SEVERAL DIFFERENT COLOR MODULES FOR THE CHARACTERS BECAUSE OF THE CONTINUALLY CHANGING ENVIRONMENTS AND LIGHT SOURCES. ARIEL'S BLUE-GREEN TAIL ON LAND WHEN SHE SAVES ERIC IS ONE OF AT LEAST THIRTY-TWO COLORS USED FOR HER CHARACTER.

DONALD'S CRIME
1945

DONALD PAYS DEARLY
FOR THIS DATE WITH
DAISY AND FOR THE
THEFT THAT MADE THE
OUTING POSSIBLE.
FILLED WITH REMORSE
FOR STEALING MONEY
FROM HIS NEPHEWS,
DONALD SUFFERS A
SERIES OF HALLUCINA-
TIONS ABOUT BEING A
GANGSTER ON THE RUN.
HE THEN WORKS THE
REST OF THE NIGHT AS A
DISHWASHER SO HE CAN
RETURN THE MISAPPRO-
PRIATED FUNDS.

PLUTO'S HEART THROB
1950

THE CURVACEOUS DACHSHUND, DINAH, FIRST APPEARED IN 1942 AS PLUTO'S LOVE INTEREST IN *THE SLEEPWALKER*. IN *PLUTO'S HEART THROB*, A CANINE CUPID CAUSES PLUTO AND DINAH TO FALL MADLY IN LOVE WITH EACH OTHER. TROUBLE BREWS WHEN PLUTO'S NEMESIS, BUTCH, ARRIVES ON THE SCENE WITH UNWELCOME ADVANCES TOWARD DINAH. THE TWO RIVALS MUST FIGHT FOR DINAH'S PAW, AND IN THE END, PLUTO'S BRAVERY AND HEROISM WIN DINAH'S HEART, AND HER UNDYING LOVE.

THE END

CINDERELLA
1950

CINDERELLA STANDS OUT AMONG
EARLY DISNEY HEROINES FOR HER
STRONG WILL AND DECISIVENESS.
NOT ONE TO LET THINGS JUST HAP-
PEN TO HER, SHE KNOWS WHEN TO
TAKE MATTERS INTO HER OWN
HANDS. THE ROYAL BALL IS THE
PERFECT EXAMPLE. SHE IS DETER-
MINED TO ATTEND DESPITE THE
OBJECTIONS OF HER STEPMOTHER
AND STEPSISTERS. HER PERSEVER-
ANCE PAYS OFF. WITH THE HELP OF
HER FAIRY GODMOTHER, SHE GOES
TO THE BALL IN STYLE. IN ONE
DANCE, PRINCE CHARMING
BECOMES COMPLETELY ENAMORED
BY CINDERELLA AND INSISTS HE
WILL MARRY NO OTHER.